Medical Terminology for Interpreters

Essential English-Spanish **MEDICAL** Terms

José Luis Leyva

Copyright © 2018 José Luis Leyva

All rights reserved – Derechos reservados

Idea Editorial – www.ideaeditorial.com

Series: Essential Technical Terminology

ISBN: 1985346176
ISBN-13: 978-1985346178

PREFACE

Being bilingual is an asset; and mastering different fields of speciality will make a difference in your bilingual skills. This book can be a helpful resource to learn the essential English-Spanish MEDICAL terms. Learn 4 to 5 terms each day and at the end of 2018 you will master the essential MEDICAL terminology in this language combination. This book contains only the most frequently used MEDICAL terminology in English and Spanish.

PREFACIO

Hablar dos idiomas es una gran ventaja; dominar diferentes campos de especialización marcará una diferencia es sus habilidades bilingües.
Este libro puede ser de gran ayuda para aprender los términos MÉDICOS esenciales en inglés y español. Aprenda 4 ó 5 términos cada día y al final del 2018 usted habrá dominado la terminología MÉDICA esencial en esta combinación de idiomas. Este libro contiene solamente la terminología MÉDICA más frecuentemente utilizada en inglés y español.

ENGLISH-SPANISH
INGLÉS-ESPAÑOL

A

abdomen, abdomen
abdominal, abdominal
abnormal, anormal
abortion, aborto
abrasion, abrasión/raspadura
abscess, absceso
abstinence, abstinencia
abuse, abuso
accident, accidente
acetaminophen, acetaminofén
ache, dolor
acid, ácido
acne, acné
active, activo

acute, agudo

addict, adicto

addiction, adicción

admit (into hospital), ingresar

adolescence, adolescencia

adopt (to), adoptar

adult, adulto

adrenaline, adrenalina

advise (to), aconsejar

afterbirth, placenta

agitation, agitación

ailment, enfermedad

air, aire

alcoholism, alcoholismo

alive, vivo

allergic, alérgico

allergy, alergia

ambulance, ambulancia

amenorrhea, amenorrea

amino acid, aminoácido

ammonia, amoníaco

amnesia, amnesia

amniocentesis, amniocentesis

amniotic sac, bolsa amniótica

amphetamines, anfetaminas

amputate (to), amputar

analgesic, analgésico

analysis, análisis

anaphylactic, shock anafiláctico

anatomy, anatomía

anemia, anemia

anemic, anémico

anesthesia, anestesia

anesthesiologist, anestesiólogo

aneurysm/aneurism, aneurisma

anger, enojo

angiogram, angiograma

angioplasty, angioplastia

anorexia, anorexia

antacid, antiácido

anthrax, ántrax

antibiotic, antibiótico

antibodies, anticuerpos

anticoagulant, anticoagulante

antidepressant, antidepresivo

antidote, antídoto

antihistamine, antihistamínico

anus, ano

anxiety, ansiedad

aorta, aorta

apathy, apatía

apnea, apnea

appendectomy, apendectomía

appendicitis, apendicitis

appetite, apetito

applicator, aplicador

appointment, cita

arm, brazo

arm pit, axila

arrhythmia, arritmia

artery, arteria

arthritis, artritis

asphyxia, asfixia

asthma, asma

asthmatic, asmático

astigmatism, astigmatismo

athlete's foot, pie de atleta

atrophy, atrofia

autism, autismo

autopsy, autopsia

awake, despierto

awaken (to), despertar

B

baby, bebé
back, espalda
backbone, columna vertebral
bacteria, bacteria
bad, malo(a)
balance, equilibrio
bald, calvo
baldness, calvicie
bandage, vendaje
bandaid, curita
barbiturates, barbitúricos
barium, bario
basin, palangana
bath, baño

bathe (to), bañarse

bed, cama

bedpan, orinal

bedridden (patient), encamado

bed-wetting, enuresis

behavior, conducta

belch, eructo

belly, vientre

bellybutton, ombligo

benign, benigno

bib, babero

biceps, bíceps

bicuspid, bicúspide

bile, bilis

bilirubin, bilirrubina

biological, biológico

biopsy, biopsia

birth, nacimiento/parto

birthmark, lunar

bite, mordedura

bite (insect), picadura

bitter, amargo

blackheads, espinillas

bladder, vejiga

bleed, sangrar

blind, ciego

blindness, ceguera

blink, parpadear

blister, ampolla

blockage, obstrucción

blood, sangre

body, cuerpo

bone, hueso

booster shot, vacuna de refuerzo

bottle, botella

botulism, botulismo

bowel, intestino

brace, aparato ortopédico

braces (dental), frenos dentales

brain, cerebro

break, quebrar

breast/chest, pecho/seno

breastbone, esternón

breath, aliento

breathe, respirar

broken, roto

bronchitis, bronquitis

bruise, moretón

bruised, amoratado
bulimia, bulimia
bulimic, bulímico
bump, protuberancia
bunion, juanete
burn, quemadura
burp, eructar
bursitis, bursitis
buttock, glúteo
buzzing, zumbido

C

calcified, calcificado
calcium, calcio
calf (of leg), pantorilla
callus, callo
calorie, caloría
cancer, cáncer
cancerous, canceroso
cane, bastón
capillary, capilar
capsule, cápsula
carbohydrate, carbohidrato
carcinogenic, carcinogénico
carcinoma, carcinoma
cardiac, cardíaco

cardiologist, cardiólogo

cardiology, cardiología

care, cuidado

cartilage, cartílago

cast, yeso

castration, castración

cataract, catarata

catatonic, catatónico

catheter, catéter

catheterization, cateterismo

catheterize, cateterizar

cause, causa

cauterize, cauterizar

cervix, cuello del útero

chafe, rozar

checkup, examen

cheek, mejilla

chemical, químico

chemotherapy, quimioterapia

chest, pecho

chew, masticar

chicken pox, varicela

childbirth, parto

childhood, infancia

chills, escalofríos
chin, barbilla
chiropractor, quiropráctico
chlamydia, clamidia
choke, ahogarse
cholera, cólera
cholesterol, colesterol
chronic, crónico
cigarette, cigarrillo
circulation, circulación
circumcision, circuncisión
cirrhosis, cirrosis
claustrophobia, claustrofobia
cleft palate, paladar hendido
clinic, clínica
clitoris, clítoris
clot, coágulo
cocaine, cocaína
coccyx, cóccix
codeine, codeína
cold, frío/a
cold (illness), resfriado común
cold sores, herpes labial
colic, cólico

colitis, colitis
collagen, colágeno
collarbone, clavícula
colon, colon
colonoscopy, colonoscopía
color-blindness, daltonismo
colostomy, colostomia
coma, coma
comatose, comatoso
comfortable, cómodo
complaint, queja
complexion, tez
complication, complicación
compress, compresa
conceive, concebir
concussion, conmoción cerebral
condom, condón
confused, confundido
confusion, confusión
congenital, congénito
congested (to be), estar congestionado
congestion, congestión
conjunctiva, conjuntiva
conjunctivitis, conjuntivitis

conscious, consciente

consciousness, conocimiento

consent, consentir

constipation, estreñimiento

contagious, contagioso

contaminated, contaminado

contraception, anticoncepción

contractions, contracciones

contusion, contusión

convalescent, convaleciente

convulsion, convulsión

corn (callus), callo

coronary, coronario

cortisone, cortisona

cough, tos

cough, toser

CPR, reanimación cardiopulmonar

crabs, ladillas

cramp, calambre

cramps (menstrual), cólicos menstruales

cranium, cráneo

craving, antojo

crawl, gatear

crib, cuna

cripple, lisiar

crippled, lisiado

critical, crítico

Crohn's disease, enfermedad de Crohn

cross-eyed, bizco

croup, crup

crutches, muletas

cry, llorar

CT scan, tomografía por computadora

culture, cultivo

cure, curar

cut, cortar

cuticle, cutícula

cyst, quiste

cystic fibrosis, fibrosis quística

D

daily, diariamente
dandruff, caspa
danger, peligro
daze, aturdimiento
dead, muerto
deaf, sordo
deaf-mute, sordomudo
deafness, sordera
death, muerte
deceased, difunto
decongestant, descongestionante
defecate, defecar
defibrillation, desfibrilación
defibrillator, desfibrilador

deficiency, deficiencia

deformed, deformado

deformity, deformidad

dehydration, deshidratación

delirious, delirante

delirium, delirio

delivery (of a baby), parto

deltoids, deltoides

dementia, demencia

dental, dental

dentist, dentista

denture, dentadura postiza

depigmentation, despigmentación

depression, depresión

dermatitis, dermatitis

dermatologist, dermatólogo

deterioration, deterioro

detoxification, desintoxicación

develop, desarrollar

diabetes, diabetes

diagnose, diagnosticar

diagnosis, diagnóstico

dialysis, diálisis

diaper, pañal

diaphragm, diafragma
diarrhea, diarrea
die, morir
diet, dieta
dietitian, dietista
digest, digerir
digestion, digestión
dilated, dilatado
dilation, dilatación
dilute, diluir
diphtheria, difteria
disability, discapacidad
discharge, secreción
discharge from hospital, dar de alta
discontinue, suspender
disease, enfermedad
disinfect, desinfectar
disinfectant, desinfectante
disk (slipped), disco desplazado
dislocation, dislocación
disorder, trastorno
disorientation, desorientación
distend, distender
distressed, angustiado

diuretic, diurético
dizziness, mareos
dizzy, mareado
doctor, médico
doctor's office, consultorio
donor, donante
dosage, dosis
double vision, vista doble
drain, supurar
draw blood, sacar sangre
dropper, gotero
drops, gotas
drowning, ahogamiento
drowsy, somnoliento
drug addiction, adicción a las drogas
drugs (usually illicit), drogas
drugs (legal), medicinas
drunk, borracho
dryness, sequedad
due date, fecha aproximada de parto
dull (pain), sordo (dolor)
duodenum, duodeno
dust, polvo
dwarfism, enanismo

dysentery, disentería

dyslexia, dislexia

dystrophy, distrofia

E

ear (inner), oído
ear (middle), oído medio
ear (outer), oreja
earache, dolor de oído
eardrum, tímpano
earlobe, lóbulo
earplugs, tapones para los oídos
eczema, eccema
edema, edema
egg, huevo/óvulo
ejaculate, eyacular
EKG, electrocardiograma
elbow, codo
elderly, anciano

electrocardiogram, electrocardiograma

electrocution, electrocución

elixir, elixir

emaciated, escuálido

embolism, embolia

embryo, embrión

emergency, emergencia

pulmonary emphysema, enfisema pulmonar

encephalitis, encefalitis

endemic, endémico

endocrine, endocrino

endocrinologist, endocrinólogo

endorphin, endorfina

endoscopy, endoscopía

enema, enema

enlargement, agrandamiento

enzyme, enzima

epidemic, epidémico/epidemia

epidural, epidural

epiglottis, epiglotis

epilepsy, epilepsia

erection, erección

esophagus, esófago

estrogen, estrógeno

ether, éter

euphoria, euforia

Eustachian tube, trompa de Eustaquio

euthanasia, eutanasia

exam, examen

examine, examinar

excrement, excremento

exercise, ejercicio

exertion, esfuerzo

exfoliation, exfoliación

exhale, exhalar

exhaustion, agotamiento

expectorant, expectorante

expert, experto

explain, explicar

exposure, exposición

external, externo

extract, extraer

extraction, extracción

eye, ojo

eyebrow, ceja

eyelash, pestaña

eyelid, párpado

eyesight, vista

F

face, cara

face down, boca abajo

face up, boca arriba

faint, desmayarse

fainting spells, desmayos

fall, caída

Fallopian tubes, trompas de Falopio

false teeth, dientes postizos

family planning, planificación familiar

fast, ayunar

fat (food), grasa

fat (person), gordo

fatal, fatal/mortal

fatigue, fatiga

fear, miedo

feces, heces

feed, alimentar

feel, sentir

feet, pies

femur, fémur

fertile, fértil

fertilization, fertilización

fetal monitor, monitor fetal

fetus, feto

fever, fiebre

fiber, fibra

fibrillation, fibrilación

filling (dental), empaste

finger, dedo (de la mano)

finger pad, yema

fire, fuego/incendio

first aid, primeros auxilios

fissure, fisura

fist, puño

flake, escama

flat foot, pie plano

flatulence, flatulencia

flexible, flexible

flu, gripe
fluoride, fluoruro
flush, rubor
foam, espuma
folic acid, ácido fólico
folk healer, curandero
follicle, folículo
follow-up, examen de seguimiento
food, alimentos
foot, pie
forceps, fórceps
forearm, antebrazo
forehead, frente
foreskin, prepucio
form, formulario
formula, fórmula
fracture, fractura
freckle, peca
freeze, congelar
frequency, frecuencia
fright, susto
function, función
fungus, hongo

G

gag, provocar náuseas

gain weight, subir de peso

gall bladder, vesícula biliar

gallstones, cálculos biliares

gangrene, gangrena

gargle, hacer gárgaras

gas, gas

gash, tajo

gastric ulcer, úlcera gástrica

gastritis, gastritis

gastroenterologist, gastroenterólogo

gastrointestinal (GI), gastrointestinal

gauze, gasa

gel, gel

gender, sexo
genes, genes
genetic, genético
genitals, genitales
geriatric, geriátrico
germ, germen
German measles, rubéola
gestation, gestación
gigantism, gigantismo
giardia, giardia
gingivitis, gingivitis
gland, glándula
glasses, gafas
glaucoma, glaucoma
glove, guante
glucose, glucosa
gluten, gluten
goiter, bocio
gonorrhea, gonorrea
goose bumps, piel de gallina
gout, gota
gown, bata
graft, injerto
gram, gramo

grief, pesar
grieve, afligirse
grind, moler
groin, ingle
growth, crecimiento
guilt, culpa
gums, encías
gun, pistola
gurney, camilla
gut, intestino/tripas
gynecologist, ginecólogo
gynecology, ginecología

H

habit, hábito

hair, pelo

hair (body), vello

halitosis, mal aliento

hallucination, alucinación

hammer, martillo de reflejos

hamstring, músculo posterior del muslo

hand, mano

hangnail, padrastro

hangover, resaca

hardening, endurecimiento

harm, dañar

harmful, dañino

harmless, inofensivo

head, cabeza

headache, dolor de cabeza

heal, curarse

health, salud

health care, atención a la salud

healthy, sano

hear, oír

hearing, audición

heart, corazón

heart attack, ataque cardíaco

heartbeat, latido del corazón

heartburn, acidez estomacal

heat-stroke, insolación

heating pad, cojín eléctrico

heel, talón

height, altura

helicopter, helicóptero

hematoma, hematoma

hemoglobin, hemoglobina

hemophilia, hemofilia

hemorrhage, hemorragia

hepatitis, hepatitis

herb, hierba

herbalist, yerbero

hereditary, hereditario
heredity, herencia
hermaphrodite, hermafrodita
hernia, hernia
heroin, heroína
herpes, herpes
heterosexual, heterosexual
hiccups, hipo
high blood pressure, presión alta
hip, cadera
hives, ronchas
hoarse, ronco
hoarseness, ronquera
homeopathy, homeopatía
homosexual, homosexual
hookworm, anquilostomosis
hormonal, hormonal
hormone, hormona
hospital, hospital
hospitalize, internar
hot flashes, sofocos
hunchback, jorobado
hurt, doler
hydrate, hidratar

hydrogen peroxide, peróxido de hidrógeno

hygiene, higiene

hymen, himen

hyperactive, hiperactivo

hyperglycemia, hiperglucemia

hypersensitivity, hipersensibilidad

hypertension, presión alta

hyperthermia, hipertermia

hyperthyroidism, hipertiroidismo

hyperventilation, hiperventilación

hypochondria, hipocondria

hypoglycemia, hipoglucemia

hypothalamus, hipotálamo

hypothermia, hipotermia

hypothyroidism, hipotiroidismo

hypoxia, hipoxia

hysterectomy, histerectomía

hysteria, histeria

I

ibuprofen, ibuprofeno
ill, enfermo
illness, enfermedad
immature, inmaduro
immobile, inmóvil
immobilization, inmovilización
immune, inmune
immunize, inmunizar
impacted tooth, diente impactado
impaired, dañado
impairment, incapacidad
implant, implantar
impotence, impotencia
impregnation, fecundación

incest, incesto

incision, incisión

incontinence, incontinencia

incubator, incubadora

incurable, incurable

indigestion, indigestión

induce, inducir

infant, bebé

infect, infectar

infection, infección

infertile, estéril

infertility, infertilidad

inflammation, inflamación

influenza, gripe

ingest, ingerir

inhale, inhalar

inhaler, inhalador

inject, inyectar

injury, lesión

inoculate, inocular

inoculation, inoculación

insane, loco

insanity, locura

insemination, inseminación

insomnia, insomnio

instrument, instrumento

insulin, insulina

insurance, seguro

intensive care, terapia intensiva

intercourse, relaciones sexuales

internal, interno

internist, internista

intestine, intestino

intoxication, intoxicación

intravenous fluids, líquidos intravenosos

intubation, intubación

iodine, yodo

iron, hierro

irregular heartbeat, latidos cardíacos irregulares

irrigate, irrigar

irritation, irritación

itch, comezón

J

jaundice, ictericia/piel amarilla

jaw, mandíbula

jelly, jalea

jock itch, tiña crural

joint, articulación

jugular, yugular

juice, jugo

K

kidney, riñón
kidney failure, insuficiencia renal
kidney stones, cálculos renales
knee, rodilla
kneecap, rótula
knife, cuchillo
knot, nudo
knuckle, nudillo

L

labor, trabajo de parto

labor pains, dolores de parto

laboratory, laboratorio

labyrinthitis, laberintitis

laceration, laceración

lactation, lactancia

lactose, lactosa

lame extremity, extremidad lisiada

language, lenguaje

laparoscopy, laparoscopía

large intestine, intestino grueso

laryngitis, laringitis

larynx, laringe

laser treatment, tratamiento con láser

latex, látex
laughing gas, gas hilarante (óxido nitroso)
laxative, laxante
lead, plomo
leech, sanguijuela
left-handed, zurdo
leg, pierna
leprosy, lepra
lesbian, lesbiana
lesion, lesión
lethargy, letargo
leukemia, leucemia
libido, deseo sexual
lice, piojos
life, vida
lifestyle, estilo de vida
ligament, ligamento
light-headedness, vahído
limb, extremidad
liniment, linimento
liposuction, liposucción
lips, labios
liquid, líquido
lisp, ceceo

listen, escuchar

live, vivir

liver, hígado

lobe, lóbulo

lobotomy, lobotomía

lockjaw, tétanos

low blood pressure, presión baja

lozenges, pastillas para la garganta

lubricate, lubricar

lump, bulto

lumpectomy, tumorectomía

lungs, pulmones

lupus, lupus

lymph, linfa

lymph nodes, ganglios linfáticos

lymphoma, linfoma

M

malabsorption, malabsorción
malaise, malestar
malaria, paludismo
male, varón/masculino
malformation, malformación
malignant, maligno
malnutrition, desnutrición
malpractice, negligencia médica
mammogram, mamografía
mania, manía
manic-depressive, maníaco depresivo
marijuana, marihuana
mask, máscara
mass, masa

massage/rub, masajear

mastectomy, mastectomía

maternal, materno

maturity, madurez

measles, sarampión

medical record, expediente médico

medication, medicamento

medicine, medicina

melanoma, melanoma

meningitis, meningitis

menopause, menopausia

menses, menstruación

menstrual cycle, ciclo menstrual

menstruation, menstruación

mental illness, trastorno mental

metabolism, metabolismo

metastasis, metástasis

methadone, metadona

methamphetamine, metanfetamina

microscope, microscopio

microsurgery, microcirugía

midwife, partera

migraine, migraña

mind, mente

miscarriage, aborto natural

mite, ácaro

mole, lunar

monitor, monitor

mononucleosis, mononucleosis

morgue, morgue

morphine, morfina

mortality, mortalidad

mouth, boca

mucous, mucoso/mucosa

mumps, paperas

muscle, músculo

mutation, mutación

mute, mudo

myopia, miopía

N

nail, uña

naked, desnudo

nap, siesta

nape, nuca

narcolepsy, narcolepsia

narcotic, narcótico

natural, natural

nausea, náuseas

navel, ombligo

nearsightedness, miopía

neck, cuello

needle, aguja

nerve, nervio

nervous, nervioso

neuralgia, neuralgia
neurologist, neurólogo
neurology, neurología
neurosis, neurosis
neurotic, neurótico
nicotine, nicotina
nightmare, pesadilla
nipple, pezón
nitroglycerine, nitroglicerina
normal, normal
nose, nariz
nostril, fosa nasal
nourishment, nutrición
numbness, adormecimiento
nurse, enfermera
nutrient, nutriente
nutrition, nutrición
nutritionist, nutricionista

O

obese, obeso
obesity, obesidad
obstetrician, obstetra
obstetrics, obstetricia
obstruction, obstrucción
occlusion, oclusión
odor, olor
office, consultorio
ointment, ungüento
oncologist, oncólogo
oncology, oncología
operate, operar
ophthalmologist, oftalmólogo,
optic, óptico

optometrist, optometrista
oral, oral
organ, órgano
orgasm, orgasmo
orthodontist, ortodoncista
orthopedics, ortopedia
orthopedist, ortopedista
osteoarthritis, osteoartritis
osteopath, osteópata
osteoporosis, osteoporosis
ovary, ovario
overdose, sobredosis
overweight, sobrepeso
ovulate, ovular
ovulation, ovulación
oxygen, oxígeno

P

pacemaker, marcapaso

pacifier, chupete

pain, dolor

pain reliever, calmante para el dolor

painful, doloroso

palate, paladar

pale, pálido

paleness, palidez

palpitations, palpitaciones

pancreas, páncreas

Pap smear, examen de Papanicolaou

paralysis, parálisis

paralyzed, paralítico

paramedic, paramédico

paranoia, paranoia
paraplegic, parapléjico
parasite, parásito
patch, parche
paternal, paterno
pathologist, patólogo
patient, paciente
pediatric, pediátrico
pediatrician, pediatra
pediatrics, pediatría
pelvis, pelvis
penetrate, penetrar
penicillin, penicilina
penis, pene
perforation, perforación
perspire, transpirar
pertussis, tos ferina
pharmacist, farmacéutico
pharmacy, farmacia
pharynx, faringe
phlegm, flema
phobia, fobia
phosphorus, fósforo
photosensitivity, fotosensibilidad

physical therapy, fisioterapia

physician, médico

pill, píldora

pillow, almohada

pimples, espinillas

placenta, placenta

plague, plaga

plaque, placa

plasma, plasma

platelets, plaquetas

pneumonia, pulmonía

podiatrist, podólogo

poison, veneno

polio, poliomielitis

pollen, polen

polyp, pólipo

pore, poro

postmenopausal, postmenopáusico

post-op, después de la operación

postpartum, posparto

potassium, potasio

pound, libra

powder, polvo

predispose, predisponer

preeclampsia, pre eclampsia
pregnancy, embarazo
pregnant, embarazada
premature birth, nacimiento prematuro
premenopausal, pre menopáusico
prenatal care, cuidado prenatal
prescribe, recetar
prescription, receta
pressure, presión
prevent, prevenir
prevention, prevención
procedure, procedimiento
proctologist, proctólogo
progesterone, progesterona
prognosis, pronóstico
prostate gland, próstata
protein, proteína
psoriasis, psoriasis
psychiatrist, psiquiatra
psychologist, psicólogo
psychosis, psicosis
psychotherapy, psicoterapia
psychotic, psicótico
puberty, pubertad

pubic hair, vello púbico

pulmonary, pulmonar

pulmonary edema, edema pulmonar

pulsating, pulsante

pulse, pulso

pump, bomba

pupil, pupila

pus, pus

Q

quadriceps, cuádriceps

quarantine, cuarentena

quinine, quinina

quota, cuota

R

rabies, rabia

radiation treatment, tratamiento de radiación

radiologist, radiólogo

radiology, radiología

radiotherapy, radioterapia

rape, violación

rash, erupción

reaction, reacción

reconstruct, reconstruir

recovery, recuperación

rectum, recto

redness, enrojecimiento

refill, rellenar

reflex, reflejo

reflux, reflujo
regurgitation, regurgitación
rehabilitate, rehabilitar
rehydrate, rehidratar
reject, rechazar
relapse, recaída
relationship (family), parentesco
relax, descansar
relief, alivio
remedy, remedio
renal failure, insuficiencia renal
replace, reemplazar
reproduce, reproducir
reproduction, reproducción
respirator, respirador
respiratory, respiratorio
rest, descansar
result, resultado
resuscitation, resucitación
retention, retención
retina, retina
revive, reanimarse
rheumatic fever, fiebre reumática
rheumatism, reumatismo

rhinoplasty, rinoplastia

rhythm method, método del ritmo

rib, costilla

rigidity, rigidez

rigor mortis, rigor mortis

risk, riesgo

rubella, rubéola

runny nose, secreción nasal

rupture, ruptura

S

safe, seguro

saline, salino

saliva, saliva

salmonella, salmonela

salt, sal

sample, muestra

sane, cuerdo

sanitary, sanitario

sanity, cordura

sarcoma, sarcoma

scab, costra

scabies, sarna

scald, escaldadura

scale, balanza

scalp, cuero cabelludo

scaly, escamoso

scar, cicatriz

scarlet fever, fiebre escarlatina

schizophrenia, esquizofrenia

sciatica, ciática

scissors, tijeras

scoliosis, escoliosis

scratch, rasguño

scream, grito

screen, examen de detección

scrotum, escroto

scurvy, escorbuto

sealant, sellador

seasickness, mareo (en un barco)

secrete, secretar

secretion, secreción

sedative, sedante

sedentary, sedentario

seizures, convulsiones

semen, semen

senile, senil

senility, senilidad

sensation, sensación

sensitive, sensible

sensitivity, sensibilidad

septum, tabique

serious, serio

serum, suero

severe, severo

sex, sexo

sexuality, sexualidad

shakes, temblores

sharp (pain), agudo (dolor)

shin, espinilla

shingles, herpes zoster

shiver, escalofríos

shiver, tiritar

shock, choque

shot, inyección

shoulder, hombro

shoulder blade, omóplato

sibling, hermano/hermana

sick, enfermo

sickness, enfermedad

side, lado

side effect, efecto secundario

sight, vista

sinus, seno paranasal

sinusitis, sinusitis

skeleton, esqueleto

skin, piel

skinny, flaco

skull, cráneo

sleep, dormir

sleeping pill, somnífero

sleepy, tener sueño

sling, cabestrillo

slip, resbalar

slipped disc, disco desplazado

sliver, astilla

slur, arrastrar las palabras

small intestine, intestino delgado

smallpox, viruela

smell, oler

smoke, fumar

snakebite, mordedura de serpiente

sneeze, estornudar

snore, roncar

soap, jabón

sober, sobrio

social worker, trabajador social

sodium, sodio
sole (of foot), planta del pie
sonogram, ecografía
sore, llaga
spasm, espasmo
specialist, especialista
specimen, muestra/espécimen
speculum, espéculo
speech pathologist, foniatra
sperm, esperma
spermicide, espermicida
sphincter, esfínter
spider bite, picadura de araña
spina bifida, espina bífida
spinal column, columna vertebral
spinal cord, médula espinal
spleen, bazo
splint, férula
splint, entablillar
splinter, astilla
sponge, esponja
spots, manchas
spotted fever, fiebre maculosa
sprain, torcedura

sprain, torcerse

sputum, esputo

stab, puñalada

stain, mancha

starvation, inanición

sterile, estéril

sterility, esterilidad

sterilize, esterilizar

sternum, esternón

steroid, esteroide

stethoscope, estetoscopio

stiff, rígido

stimulant, estimulante

sting, picadura de insecto

sting, picar

stirrup, estribo

stitches, puntos de suturas

stoma, estoma

stomach, estómago

stomach ache/pain, dolor de estómago

stool, excremento

strangle, estrangular

strength, fuerza

strep, estreptococo

stress, estrés
stretch mark, estría
stretcher, camilla
stroke, derrame cerebral
strong, fuerte
stuffy nose, nariz tapada
stupor, estupor
stutter, tartamudear
suffocation, sofocación
suicide, suicidio
sunburn, quemadura por el sol
sunstroke, insolación
suppository, supositorio
surgeon, cirujano
surgery, cirugía
surrogate mother, madre portadora
survive, sobrevivir
suture, sutura
swab, hisopo
swallow, tragar
sweat, sudor
swelling, hinchazón
swollen, hinchado
symptom, síntoma

syndrome, síndrome

synthetic, sintético

syphilis, sífilis

syringe, jeringa

syrup, jarabe

T

table, mesa

tablespoonful, cucharada

tablet, tableta

tailbone, cóccix

take, tomar

talcum powder, talco

tampon, tampón

tapeworm, teniasis

taste, sabor

taste bud, papila gustativa

tattoo, tatuaje

tear (of muscle/ligament), desgarro

tear (of the eye), lágrima

teaspoonful, cucharadita

technician, técnico

temperature, temperatura

temple (of the head), sien

temporary, temporal

tender, adolorido

tendinitis, tendinitis

tendon, tendón

terminal, terminal

test, prueba/examen

testicles, testículos

testosterone, testosterona

tetanus, tétano

therapist, terapeuta

therapy, terapia

thermometer, termómetro

thick, espeso (consistency)/grueso (dimension)

thigh, muslo

thirst, sed

thirsty (to be), tener sed

thorax, tórax

throat, garganta

throbbing, pulsante

thrombosis, trombosis

throw up, vomitar

thumb, pulgar

thyroid gland, glándula tiroides

tincture, tintura

tingling, hormigueo

tinnitus, zumbido en los oídos

tissue, tejido

tobacco, tabaco

toe, dedo del pie

toilet, inodoro

tolerate, tolerar

tongue, lengua

tonic, tónico

tonsil, amígdala

tonsillectomy, amigdalectomía

tonsillitis, amigdalitis

tooth, diente

toothache, dolor de muelas

touch, tocar

tourniquet, torniquete

towel, toalla

toxemia, toxemia

toxic, tóxico

toxin, toxina

trace, rastro

trachea, traquea

traction, tracción

tranquilizers, tranquilizantes

transfusion, transfusión

transmitted, transmitido

transplant, trasplantar

trauma, trauma

traumatic, traumático

treat, tratar

treatment, tratamiento

tremors, temblores

triceps, tríceps

trouble, molestia

tube, tubo

tuberculosis, tuberculosis

tumor, tumor

tweezers, pinzas

twin, gemelo

twisted, torcido

typhoid fever, fiebre tifoidea

typhus, tifus

U

ulcer, úlcera
ultrasound, ultrasonido
umbilical cord, cordón umbilical
uncomfortable, incómodo
unconscious, inconsciente
unhealthy, insalubre
unstable, inestable
urethra, uretra
urgent, urgente
urinal, orinal
urinalysis, examen general de orina
urinary, urinario
urinate, orinar
urine, orina

urine sample, muestra de orina

urologist, urólogo

urology, urología

uterus, útero

V

vaccinate, vacunar
vaccine, vacuna
vagina, vagina
vaginal, vaginal
vaginitis, vaginitis
valve, válvula
varicose vein, vena varicosa
vascular, vascular
vasectomy, vasectomía
vegetative, vegetativo
vein, vena
venereal disease, enfermedad venérea
venom, veneno
ventilator, ventilador

ventricle, ventrículo

vertebrae, vértebras

vertigo, vértigo

victim, víctima

virile, viril

virus, virus

vision, vista

visiting hours, horario de visita

vital, vital

vital organ, órgano vital

vital signs, signos vitales

vitamin, vitamina

vocal cord, cuerda vocal

vomit, vomitar

W

waist, cintura
waiting room, sala de espera
wake up, despertar
walker, andador
ward, sala
warning, aviso
wart, verruga
wash (to), lavar
water, agua
watery eyes, ojos llorosos
weak, débil
weakness, debilidad
wean, destetar
weary, fatigado

weigh, pesar
weight, peso
weight change, cambio de peso
wet nurse, nodriza
wheel chair, silla de ruedas
wheeze, sibilancia
wheeze, respirar con sibilancias
white blood cells, glóbulos blancos
whooping cough (pertussis), tos ferina
windpipe, tráquea
wisdom tooth, muela del juicio
womb, útero
worms (intestinal), lombrices
wound, herida
wrist, muñeca

X

x-rays, radiografías/rayos X

Y

yawn, bostezar

SPANISH-ENGLISH
ESPAÑOL-INGLÉS

A

abdomen, abdomen

abdominal, abdominal

aborto, abortion

aborto natural, miscarriage

abrasión/raspadura, abrasion

absceso, abscess

abstinencia, abstinence

abuso, abuse

ácaro, mite

accidente, accident

acetaminofén, acetaminophen

acidez estomacal, heartburn

ácido, acid

ácido fólico, folic acid

acné, acne

aconsejar, advise (to)

activo, active

adicción, addiction

adicción a las drogas, drug addiction

adicto, addict

adolescencia, adolescence

adolorido, tender

adoptar, adopt (to)

adormecimiento, numbness

adrenalina, adrenaline

adulto, adult

afligirse, grieve

agitación, agitation

agotamiento, exhaustion

agrandamiento, enlargement

agua, water

agudo, acute

agudo (dolor), sharp (pain)

aguja, needle

ahogamiento, drowning

ahogarse, choke

aire, air

alcoholismo, alcoholism

alergia, allergy
alérgico, allergic
aliento, breath
alimentar, feed
alimentos, food
alivio, relief
almohada, pillow
altura, height
alucinación, hallucination
amargo, bitter
ambulancia, ambulance
amenorrea, amenorrhea
amígdala, tonsil
amigdalectomía, tonsillectomy
amigdalitis, tonsillitis
aminoácido, amino acid
amnesia, amnesia
amniocentesis, amniocentesis
amoníaco, ammonia
amoratado, bruised
ampolla, blister
amputar, amputate (to)
analgésico, analgesic
análisis, analysis

anatomía, anatomy

anciano, elderly

andador, walker

anemia, anemia

anémico, anemic

anestesia, anesthesia

anestesiólogo, anesthesiologist

aneurisma, aneurysm/aneurism

anfetaminas, amphetamines

angiograma, angiogram

angioplastia, angioplasty

angustiado, distressed

ano, anus

anorexia, anorexia

anormal, abnormal

anquilostomosis, hookworm

ansiedad, anxiety

antebrazo, forearm

antiácido, antacid

antibiótico, antibiotic

anticoagulante, anticoagulant

anticoncepción, contraception

anticuerpos, antibodies

antidepresivo, antidepressant

antídoto, antidote

antihistamínico, antihistamine

antojo, craving

ántrax, anthrax

aorta, aorta

aparato ortopédico, brace

apatía, apathy

apendectomía, appendectomy

apendicitis, appendicitis

apetito, appetite

aplicador, applicator

apnea, apnea

arrastrar las palabras, slur

arritmia, arrhythmia

arteria, artery

articulación, joint

artritis, arthritis

asfixia, asphyxia

asma, asthma

asmático, asthmatic

astigmatismo, astigmatism

astilla, sliver

astilla, splinter

ataque cardíaco, heart attack

atención a la salud, health care

atrofia, atrophy

aturdimiento, daze

audición, hearing

autismo, autism

autopsia, autopsy

aviso, warning

axila, arm pit

ayunar, fast

B

babero, bib

bacteria, bacteria

balanza, scale

bañarse, bathe (to)

baño, bath

barbilla, chin

barbitúricos, barbiturates

bario, barium

bastón, cane

bata, gown

bazo, spleen

bebé, baby

bebé, infant

benigno, benign

bíceps, biceps
bicúspide, bicuspid
bilirrubina, bilirubin
bilis, bile
biológico, biological
biopsia, biopsy
bizco, cross-eyed
boca, mouth
boca abajo, face down
boca arriba, face up
bocio, goiter
bolsa amniótica, amniotic sac
bomba, pump
borracho, drunk
bostezar, yawn
botella, bottle
botulismo, botulism
brazo, arm
bronquitis, bronchitis
bulimia, bulimia
bulímico, bulimic
bulto, lump
bursitis, bursitis

C

cabestrillo, sling

cabeza, head

cadera, hip

caída, fall

calambre, cramp

calcificado, calcified

calcio, calcium

cálculos biliares, gallstones

cálculos renales, kidney stones

callo, callus

callo, corn (callus)

calmante para el dolor, pain reliever

caloría, calorie

calvicie, baldness

calvo, bald

cama, bed

cambio de peso, weight change

camilla, gurney

camilla, stretcher

cáncer, cancer

canceroso, cancerous

capilar, capillary

cápsula, capsule

cara, face

carbohidrato, carbohydrate

carcinogénico, carcinogenic

carcinoma, carcinoma

cardíaco, cardiac

cardiología, cardiology

cardiólogo, cardiologist

cartílago, cartilage

caspa, dandruff

castración, castration

catarata, cataract

catatónico, catatonic

catéter, catheter

cateterismo, catheterization

cateterizar, catheterize

causa, cause
cauterizar, cauterize
ceceo, lisp
ceguera, blindness
ceja, eyebrow
cerebro, brain
choque, shock
cicatriz, scar
ciclo menstrual, menstrual cycle
ciego, blind
cigarrillo, cigarette
cintura, waist
circulación, circulation
circuncisión, circumcision
cirrosis, cirrhosis
cirugía, surgery
cirujano, surgeon
cita, appointment
clamidia, chlamydia
claustrofobia, claustrophobia
clavícula, collarbone
clínica, clinic
clítoris, clitoris
coágulo, clot

cocaína, cocaine

cóccix, coccyx

cóccix, tailbone

codeína, codeine

codo, elbow

cojín eléctrico, heating pad

colágeno, collagen

cólera, cholera

colesterol, cholesterol

cólico, colic

cólicos menstruales, cramps (menstrual)

colitis, colitis

colon, colon

colonoscopía, colonoscopy

colostomia, colostomy

columna vertebral, backbone

columna vertebral, spinal column

coma, coma

comatoso, comatose

comezón, itch

cómodo, comfortable

complicación, complication

compresa, compress

concebir, conceive

condón, condom
conducta, behavior
confundido, confused
confusión, confusion
congelar, freeze
congénito, congenital
congestión, congestion
conjuntiva, conjunctiva
conjuntivitis, conjunctivitis
conmoción cerebral, concussion
conocimiento, consciousness
consciente, conscious
consentir, consent
consultorio, doctor's office
consultorio, office
contagioso, contagious
contaminado, contaminated
contracciones, contractions
contusión, contusion
convaleciente, convalescent
convulsión, convulsion
convulsiones, seizures
corazón, heart
cordón umbilical, umbilical cord

cordura, sanity

coronario, coronary

cortar, cut

cortisona, cortisone

costilla, rib

costra, scab

cráneo, cranium

cráneo, skull

crecimiento, growth

crítico, critical

crónico, chronic

crup, croup

cuádriceps, quadriceps

cuarentena, quarantine

cucharada, tablespoonful

cucharadita, teaspoonful

cuchillo, knife

cuello, neck

cuello del útero, cervix

cuerda vocal, vocal cord

cuerdo, sane

cuero cabelludo, scalp

cuerpo, body

cuidado, care

cuidado prenatal, prenatal care

culpa, guilt

cultivo, culture

cuna, crib

cuota, quota

curandero, folk healer

curar, cure

curarse, heal

curita, bandaid

cutícula, cuticle

CH

chupete, pacifier

ciática, sciatica

D

daltonismo, color-blindness
dañado, impaired
dañar, harm
dañino, harmful
dar de alta, discharge from hospital
débil, weak
debilidad, weakness
dedo (de la mano), finger
dedo del pie, toe
defecar, defecate
deficiencia, deficiency
deformado, deformed
deformidad, deformity
delirante, delirious

delirio, delirium

deltoides, deltoids

demencia, dementia

dentadura postiza, denture

dental, dental

dentista, dentist

depresión, depression

dermatitis, dermatitis

dermatólogo, dermatologist

derrame cerebral, stroke

desarrollar, develop

descansar, relax

descansar, rest

descongestionante, decongestant

deseo sexual, libido

desfibrilación, defibrillation

desfibrilador, defibrillator

desgarro, tear (of muscle/ligament)

deshidratación, dehydration

desinfectante, disinfectant

desinfectar, disinfect

desintoxicación, detoxification

desmayarse, faint

desmayos, fainting spells

desnudo, naked
desnutrición, malnutrition
desorientación, disorientation
despertar, awaken (to)
despertar, wake up
despierto, awake
despigmentación, depigmentation
después de la operación, post-op
destetar, wean
deterioro, deterioration
diabetes, diabetes
diafragma, diaphragm
diagnosticar, diagnose
diagnóstico, diagnosis
diálisis, dialysis
diariamente, daily
diarrea, diarrhea
diente, tooth
diente impactado, impacted tooth
dientes postizos, false teeth
dieta, diet
dietista, dietitian
difteria, diphtheria
difunto, deceased

digerir, digest

digestión, digestion

dilatación, dilation

dilatado, dilated

diluir, dilute

discapacidad, disability

disco desplazado, disk (slipped)

disco desplazado, slipped disc

disentería, dysentery

dislexia, dyslexia

dislocación, dislocation

distender, distend

distrofia, dystrophy

diurético, diuretic

doler, hurt

dolor, ache

dolor, pain

dolor de cabeza, headache

dolor de estómago, stomach ache/pain

dolor de muelas, toothache

dolor de oído, earache

dolores de parto, labor pains

doloroso, painful

donante, donor

dormir, sleep

dosis, dosage

drogas, drugs (usually illicit)

duodeno, duodenum

E

eccema, eczema

ecografía, sonogram

edema, edema

edema pulmonar, pulmonary edema

efecto secundario, side effect

ejercicio, exercise

electrocardiograma, EKG

electrocardiograma, electrocardiogram

electrocución, electrocution

elixir, elixir

embarazada, pregnant

embarazo, pregnancy

embolia, embolism

embrión, embryo

emergencia, emergency

empaste, filling (dental)

enanismo, dwarfism

encamado, bedridden (patient)

encefalitis, encephalitis

encías, gums

endémico, endemic

endocrino, endocrine

endocrinólogo, endocrinologist

endorfina, endorphin

endoscopía, endoscopy

endurecimiento, hardening

enema, enema

enfermedad, ailment

enfermedad, disease

enfermedad, illness

enfermedad, sickness

enfermedad de Crohn, Crohn's disease

enfermedad venérea, venereal disease

enfermera, nurse

enfermo, ill

enfermo, sick

enfisema pulmonar, pulmonary emphysema

enojo, anger

enrojecimiento, redness

entablillar, splint

enuresis, bed-wetting

enzima, enzyme

epidémico/epidemia, epidemic

epidural, epidural

epiglotis, epiglottis

epilepsia, epilepsy

equilibrio, balance

erección, erection

eructar, burp

eructo, belch

erupción, rash

escaldadura, scald

escalofríos, chills

escalofríos, shiver

escama, flake

escamoso, scaly

escoliosis, scoliosis

escorbuto, scurvy

escroto, scrotum

escuálido, emaciated

escuchar, listen

esfínter, sphincter

esfuerzo, exertion
esófago, esophagus
espalda, back
espasmo, spasm
especialista, specialist
espéculo, speculum
esperma, sperm
espermicida, spermicide
espeso (consistency)/grueso (dimension), thick
espina bífida, spina bifida
espinilla, shin
espinillas, blackheads
espinillas, pimples
esponja, sponge
espuma, foam
esputo, sputum
esqueleto, skeleton
esquizofrenia, schizophrenia
estar congestionado, congested (to be)
estéril, infertile
estéril, sterile
esterilidad, sterility
esterilizar, sterilize
esternón, breastbone

esternón, sternum

esteroide, steroid

estetoscopio, stethoscope

estilo de vida, lifestyle

estimulante, stimulant

estoma, stoma

estómago, stomach

estornudar, sneeze

estrangular, strangle

estreñimiento, constipation

estreptococo, strep

estrés, stress

estría, stretch mark

estribo, stirrup

estrógeno, estrogen

estupor, stupor

éter, ether

euforia, euphoria

eutanasia, euthanasia

examen, checkup

examen, exam

examen de detección, screen

examen de Papanicolaou, Pap smear

examen de seguimiento, follow-up

examen general de orina, urinalysis
examinar, examine
excremento, excrement
excremento, stool
exfoliación, exfoliation
exhalar, exhale
expectorante, expectorant
expediente médico, medical record
experto, expert
explicar, explain
exposición, exposure
externo, external
extracción, extraction
extraer, extract
extremidad, limb
extremidad lisiada, lame extremity
eyacular, ejaculate

F

faringe, pharynx

farmacéutico, pharmacist

farmacia, pharmacy

fatal/mortal, fatal

fatiga, fatigue

fatigado, weary

fecha aproximada de parto, due date

fecundación, impregnation

fémur, femur

fértil, fertile

fertilización, fertilization

férula, splint

feto, fetus

fibra, fiber

fibrilación, fibrillation
fibrosis quística, cystic fibrosis
fiebre, fever
fiebre escarlatina, scarlet fever
fiebre maculosa, spotted fever
fiebre reumática, rheumatic fever
fiebre tifoidea, typhoid fever
fisioterapia, physical therapy
fisura, fissure
flaco, skinny
flatulencia, flatulence
flema, phlegm
flexible, flexible
fluoruro, fluoride
fobia, phobia
folículo, follicle
foniatra, speech pathologist
fórceps, forceps
fórmula, formula
formulario, form
fosa nasal, nostril
fósforo, phosphorus
fotosensibilidad, photosensitivity
fractura, fracture

frecuencia, frequency

frenos dentales, braces (dental)

frente, forehead

frío/a, cold

fuego/incendio, fire

fuerte, strong

fuerza, strength

fumar, smoke

función, function

G

gafas, glasses
ganglios linfáticos, lymph nodes
gangrena, gangrene
garganta, throat
gas, gas
gas hilarante (óxido nitroso), laughing gas
gasa, gauze
gastritis, gastritis
gastroenterólogo, gastroenterologist
gastrointestinal, gastrointestinal (GI)
gatear, crawl
gel, gel
gemelo, twin
genes, genes

genético, genetic

genitales, genitals

geriátrico, geriatric

germen, germ

gestación, gestation

giardia, giardia

gigantismo, gigantism

ginecología, gynecology

ginecólogo, gynecologist

gingivitis, gingivitis

glándula, gland

glándula tiroides, thyroid gland

glaucoma, glaucoma

glóbulos blancos, white blood cells

glucosa, glucose

gluten, gluten

glúteo, buttock

gonorrea, gonorrhea

gordo, fat (person)

gota, gout

gotas, drops

gotero, dropper

gramo, gram

grasa, fat (food)

gripe, flu
gripe, influenza
grito, scream
guante, glove

H

hábito, habit

hacer gárgaras, gargle

heces, feces

helicóptero, helicopter

hematoma, hematoma

hemofilia, hemophilia

hemoglobina, hemoglobin

hemorragia, hemorrhage

hepatitis, hepatitis

hereditario, hereditary

herencia, heredity

herida, wound

hermafrodita, hermaphrodite

hermano/hermana, sibling

hernia, hernia
heroína, heroin
herpes, herpes
herpes labial, cold sores
herpes zoster, shingles
heterosexual, heterosexual
hidratar, hydrate
hierba, herb
hierro, iron
hígado, liver
higiene, hygiene
himen, hymen
hinchado, swollen
hinchazón, swelling
hiperactivo, hyperactive
hiperglucemia, hyperglycemia
hipersensibilidad, hypersensitivity
hipertermia, hyperthermia
hipertiroidismo, hyperthyroidism
hiperventilación, hyperventilation
hipo, hiccups
hipocondria, hypochondria
hipoglucemia, hypoglycemia
hipotálamo, hypothalamus

hipotermia, hypothermia

hipotiroidismo, hypothyroidism

hipoxia, hypoxia

hisopo, swab

histerectomía, hysterectomy

histeria, hysteria

hombro, shoulder

homeopatía, homeopathy

homosexual, homosexual

hongo, fungus

horario de visita, visiting hours

hormigueo, tingling

hormona, hormone

hormonal, hormonal

hospital, hospital

hueso, bone

huevo/óvulo, egg

I

ibuprofeno, ibuprofen

ictericia/piel amarilla, jaundice

implantar, implant

impotencia, impotence

inanición, starvation

incapacidad, impairment

incesto, incest

incisión, incision

incómodo, uncomfortable

inconsciente, unconscious

incontinencia, incontinence

incubadora, incubator

incurable, incurable

indigestión, indigestion

inducir, induce
inestable, unstable
infancia, childhood
infección, infection
infectar, infect
infertilidad, infertility
inflamación, inflammation
ingerir, ingest
ingle, groin
ingresar, admit (into hospital)
inhalador, inhaler
inhalar, inhale
injerto, graft
inmaduro, immature
inmóvil, immobile
inmovilización, immobilization
inmune, immune
inmunizar, immunize
inoculación, inoculation
inocular, inoculate
inodoro, toilet
inofensivo, harmless
insalubre, unhealthy
inseminación, insemination

insolación, heat-stroke
insolación, sunstroke
insomnio, insomnia
instrumento, instrument
insuficiencia renal, kidney failure
insuficiencia renal, renal failure
insulina, insulin
internar, hospitalize
internista, internist
interno, internal
intestino, bowel
intestino, intestine
intestino delgado, small intestine
intestino grueso, large intestine
intestino/tripas, gut
intoxicación, intoxication
intubación, intubation
inyección, shot
inyectar, inject
irrigar, irrigate
irritación, irritation

J

jabón, soap

jalea, jelly

jarabe, syrup

jeringa, syringe

jorobado, hunchback

juanete, bunion

jugo, juice

L

laberintitis, labyrinthitis
labios, lips
laboratorio, laboratory
laceración, laceration
lactancia, lactation
lactosa, lactose
ladillas, crabs
lado, side
lágrima, tear (of the eye)
laparoscopía, laparoscopy
laringe, larynx
laringitis, laryngitis
látex, latex
latido del corazón, heartbeat

latidos cardíacos irregulares, irregular heartbeat

lavar, wash (to)

laxante, laxative

lengua, tongue

lenguaje, language

lepra, leprosy

lesbiana, lesbian

lesión, injury

lesión, lesion

letargo, lethargy

leucemia, leukemia

libra, pound

ligamento, ligament

linfa, lymph

linfoma, lymphoma

linimento, liniment

liposucción, liposuction

líquido, liquid

líquidos intravenosos, intravenous fluids

lisiado, crippled

lisiar, cripple

llaga, sore

llorar, cry

lobotomía, lobotomy

lóbulo, earlobe

lóbulo, lobe

loco, insane

locura, insanity

lombrices, worms (intestinal)

lubricar, lubricate

lunar, birthmark

lunar, mole

lupus, lupus

M

madre portadora, surrogate mother

madurez, maturity

mal aliento, halitosis

malabsorción, malabsorption

malestar, malaise

malformación, malformation

maligno, malignant

malo(a), bad

mamografía, mammogram

mancha, stain

manchas, spots

mandíbula, jaw

manía, mania

maníaco depresivo, manic-depressive

mano, hand
marcapaso, pacemaker
mareado, dizzy
mareo (en un barco), seasickness
mareos, dizziness
marihuana, marijuana
martillo de reflejos, hammer
masa, mass
masajear, massage/rub
máscara, mask
mastectomía, mastectomy
masticar, chew
materno, maternal
medicamento, medication
medicina, medicine
medicinas, drugs (legal)
médico, doctor
médico, physician
médula espinal, spinal cord
mejilla, cheek
melanoma, melanoma
meningitis, meningitis
menopausia, menopause
menstruación, menses

menstruación, menstruation

mente, mind

mesa, table

metabolismo, metabolism

metadona, methadone

metanfetamina, methamphetamine

metástasis, metastasis

método del ritmo, rhythm method

microcirugía, microsurgery

microscopio, microscope

miedo, fear

migraña, migraine

miopía, myopia

miopía, nearsightedness

moler, grind

molestia, trouble

monitor, monitor

monitor fetal, fetal monitor

mononucleosis, mononucleosis

mordedura, bite

mordedura de serpiente, snakebite

moretón, bruise

morfina, morphine

morgue, morgue

morir, die
mortalidad, mortality
mucoso/mucosa, mucous
mudo, mute
muela del juicio, wisdom tooth
muerte, death
muerto, dead
muestra, sample
muestra de orina, urine sample
muestra/espécimen, specimen
muletas, crutches
muñeca, wrist
músculo, muscle
músculo posterior del muslo, hamstring
muslo, thigh
mutación, mutation

N

nacimiento prematuro, premature birth

nacimiento/parto, birth

narcolepsia, narcolepsy

narcótico, narcotic

nariz, nose

nariz tapada, stuffy nose

natural, natural

náuseas, nausea

negligencia médica, malpractice

nervio, nerve

nervioso, nervous

neuralgia, neuralgia

neurología, neurology

neurólogo, neurologist

neurosis, neurosis

neurótico, neurotic

nicotina, nicotine

nitroglicerina, nitroglycerine

nodriza, wet nurse

normal, normal

nuca, nape

nudillo, knuckle

nudo, knot

nutrición, nourishment

nutrición, nutrition

nutricionista, nutritionist

nutriente, nutrient

O

obesidad, obesity

obeso, obese

obstetra, obstetrician

obstetricia, obstetrics

obstrucción, blockage

obstrucción, obstruction

oclusión, occlusion

oftalmólogo, ophthalmologist

oído, ear (inner)

oído medio, ear (middle)

oír, hear

ojo, eye

ojos llorosos, watery eyes

oler, smell

olor, odor

ombligo, bellybutton

ombligo, navel

omóplato, shoulder blade

oncología, oncology

oncólogo, oncologist

operar, operate

óptico, optic

optometrista, optometrist

oral, oral

oreja, ear (outer)

órgano, organ

órgano vital, vital organ

orgasmo, orgasm

orina, urine

orinal, bedpan

orinal, urinal

orinar, urinate

ortodoncista, orthodontist

ortopedia, orthopedics

ortopedista, orthopedist

osteoartritis, osteoarthritis

osteópata, osteopath

osteoporosis, osteoporosis

ovario, ovary

ovulación, ovulation

ovular, ovulate

oxígeno, oxygen

P

paciente, patient
padrastro, hangnail
paladar, palate
paladar hendido, cleft palate
palangana, basin
palidez, paleness
pálido, pale
palpitaciones, palpitations
paludismo, malaria
páncreas, pancreas
pantorilla, calf (of leg)
pañal, diaper
paperas, mumps
papila gustativa, taste bud

parálisis, paralysis
paralítico, paralyzed
paramédico, paramedic
paranoia, paranoia
parapléjico, paraplegic
parásito, parasite
parche, patch
parentesco, relationship (family)
parpadear, blink
párpado, eyelid
partera, midwife
parto, childbirth
parto, delivery (of a baby)
pastillas para la garganta, lozenges
paterno, paternal
patólogo, pathologist
peca, freckle
pecho, chest
pecho/seno, breast/chest
pediatra, pediatrician
pediatría, pediatrics
pediátrico, pediatric
peligro, danger
pelo, hair

pelvis, pelvis
pene, penis
penetrar, penetrate
penicilina, penicillin
perforación, perforation
peróxido de hidrógeno, hydrogen peroxide
pesadilla, nightmare
pesar, grief
pesar, weigh
peso, weight
pestaña, eyelash
pezón, nipple
picadura, bite (insect)
picadura de araña, spider bite
picadura de insecto, sting
picar, sting
pie, foot
pie de atleta, athlete's foot
pie plano, flat foot
piel, skin
piel de gallina, goose bumps
pierna, leg
pies, feet
píldora, pill

pinzas, tweezers

piojos, lice

pistola, gun

placa, plaque

placenta, afterbirth

placenta, placenta

plaga, plague

planificación familiar, family planning

planta del pie, sole (of foot)

plaquetas, platelets

plasma, plasma

plomo, lead

podólogo, podiatrist

polen, pollen

poliomielitis, polio

pólipo, polyp

polvo, dust

polvo, powder

poro, pore

posparto, postpartum

postmenopáusico, postmenopausal

potasio, potassium

pre eclampsia, preeclampsia

pre menopáusico, premenopausal

predisponer, predispose
prepucio, foreskin
presión, pressure
presión alta, high blood pressure
presión alta, hypertension
presión baja, low blood pressure
prevención, prevention
prevenir, prevent
primeros auxilios, first aid
procedimiento, procedure
proctólogo, proctologist
progesterona, progesterone
pronóstico, prognosis
próstata, prostate gland
proteína, protein
protuberancia, bump
provocar náuseas, gag
prueba/examen, test
psicólogo, psychologist
psicosis, psychosis
psicoterapia, psychotherapy
psicótico, psychotic
psiquiatra, psychiatrist
psoriasis, psoriasis

pubertad, puberty

pulgar, thumb

pulmonar, pulmonary

pulmones, lungs

pulmonía, pneumonia

pulsante, pulsating

pulsante, throbbing

pulso, pulse

puntos de suturas, stitches

puñalada, stab

puño, fist

pupila, pupil

pus, pus

Q

quebrar, break
queja, complaint
quemadura, burn
quemadura por el sol, sunburn
químico, chemical
quimioterapia, chemotherapy
quinina, quinine
quiropráctico, chiropractor
quiste, cyst

R

rabia, rabies
radiografías/rayos X, x-rays
radiología, radiology
radiólogo, radiologist
radioterapia, radiotherapy
rasguño, scratch
rastro, trace
reacción, reaction
reanimación cardiopulmonar, CPR
reanimarse, revive
recaída, relapse
receta, prescription
recetar, prescribe
rechazar, reject

reconstruir, reconstruct
recto, rectum
recuperación, recovery
reemplazar, replace
reflejo, reflex
reflujo, reflux
regurgitación, regurgitation
rehabilitar, rehabilitate
rehidratar, rehydrate
relaciones sexuales, intercourse
rellenar, refill
remedio, remedy
reproducción, reproduction
reproducir, reproduce
resaca, hangover
resbalar, slip
resfriado común, cold (illness)
respirador, respirator
respirar, breathe
respirar con sibilancias, wheeze
respiratorio, respiratory
resucitación, resuscitation
resultado, result
retención, retention

retina, retina

reumatismo, rheumatism

riesgo, risk

rigidez, rigidity

rígido, stiff

rigor mortis, rigor mortis

rinoplastia, rhinoplasty

riñón, kidney

rodilla, knee

roncar, snore

ronchas, hives

ronco, hoarse

ronquera, hoarseness

roto, broken

rótula, kneecap

rozar, chafe

rubéola, German measles

rubéola, rubella

rubor, flush

ruptura, rupture

S

sabor, taste

sacar sangre, draw blood

sal, salt

sala, ward

sala de espera, waiting room

salino, saline

saliva, saliva

salmonela, salmonella

salud, health

sangrar, bleed

sangre, blood

sanguijuela, leech

sanitario, sanitary

sano, healthy

sarampión, measles

sarcoma, sarcoma

sarna, scabies

secreción, discharge

secreción, secretion

secreción nasal, runny nose

secretar, secrete

sed, thirst

sedante, sedative

sedentario, sedentary

seguro, insurance

seguro, safe

sellador, sealant

semen, semen

senil, senile

senilidad, senility

seno paranasal, sinus

sensación, sensation

sensibilidad, sensitivity

sensible, sensitive

sentir, feel

sequedad, dryness

serio, serious

severo, severe

sexo, gender
sexo, sex
sexualidad, sexuality
shock anafiláctico, anaphylactic
sibilancia, wheeze
sien, temple (of the head)
siesta, nap
sífilis, syphilis
signos vitales, vital signs
silla de ruedas, wheel chair
síndrome, syndrome
sintético, synthetic
síntoma, symptom
sinusitis, sinusitis
sobredosis, overdose
sobrepeso, overweight
sobrevivir, survive
sobrio, sober
sodio, sodium
sofocación, suffocation
sofocos, hot flashes
somnífero, sleeping pill
somnoliento, drowsy
sordera, deafness

sordo, deaf

sordo (dolor), dull (pain)

sordomudo, deaf-mute

subir de peso, gain weight

sudor, sweat

suero, serum

suicidio, suicide

supositorio, suppository

supurar, drain

suspender, discontinue

susto, fright

sutura, suture

T

tabaco, tobacco

tabique, septum

tableta, tablet

tajo, gash

talco, talcum powder

talón, heel

tampón, tampon

tapones para los oídos, earplugs

tartamudear, stutter

tatuaje, tattoo

técnico, technician

tejido, tissue

temblores, shakes

temblores, tremors

temperatura, temperature

temporal, temporary

tendinitis, tendinitis

tendón, tendon

tener sed, thirsty (to be)

tener sueño, sleepy

teniasis, tapeworm

terapeuta, therapist

terapia, therapy

terapia intensiva, intensive care

terminal, terminal

termómetro, thermometer

testículos, testicles

testosterona, testosterone

tétano, tetanus

tétanos, lockjaw

tez, complexion

tifus, typhus

tijeras, scissors

tímpano, eardrum

tintura, tincture

tiña crural, jock itch

tiritar, shiver

toalla, towel

tocar, touch

tolerar, tolerate

tomar, take

tomografía por computadora, CT scan

tónico, tonic

tórax, thorax

torcedura, sprain

torcerse, sprain

torcido, twisted

torniquete, tourniquet

tos, cough

tos ferina, pertussis

tos ferina, whooping cough (pertussis)

toser, cough

toxemia, toxemia

tóxico, toxic

toxina, toxin

trabajador social, social worker

trabajo de parto, labor

tracción, traction

tragar, swallow

tranquilizantes, tranquilizers

transfusión, transfusion

transmitido, transmitted

transpirar, perspire

traquea, trachea

tráquea, windpipe

trasplantar, transplant

trastorno, disorder

trastorno mental, mental illness

tratamiento, treatment

tratamiento con láser, laser treatment

tratamiento de radiación, radiation treatment

tratar, treat

trauma, trauma

traumático, traumatic

tríceps, triceps

trombosis, thrombosis

trompa de Eustaquio, Eustachian tube

trompas de Falopio, Fallopian tubes

tuberculosis, tuberculosis

tubo, tube

tumor, tumor

tumorectomía, lumpectomy

U

úlcera, ulcer
úlcera gástrica, gastric ulcer
ultrasonido, ultrasound
ungüento, ointment
uña, nail
uretra, urethra
urgente, urgent
urinario, urinary
urología, urology
urólogo, urologist
útero, uterus
útero, womb

V

vacuna, vaccine

vacuna de refuerzo, booster shot

vacunar, vaccinate

vagina, vagina

vaginal, vaginal

vaginitis, vaginitis

vahído, light-headedness

válvula, valve

varicela, chicken pox

varón/masculino, male

vascular, vascular

vasectomía, vasectomy

vegetativo, vegetative

vejiga, bladder

vello, hair (body)
vello púbico, pubic hair
vena, vein
vena varicosa, varicose vein
vendaje, bandage
veneno, poison
veneno, venom
ventilador, ventilator
ventrículo, ventricle
verruga, wart
vértebras, vertebrae
vértigo, vertigo
vesícula biliar, gall bladder
víctima, victim
vida, life
vientre, belly
violación, rape
viril, virile
viruela, smallpox
virus, virus
vista, eyesight
vista, sight
vista, vision
vista doble, double vision

vital, vital

vitamina, vitamin

vivir, live

vivo, alive

vomitar, throw up

vomitar, vomit

Y

yema, finger pad

yerbero, herbalist

yeso, cast

yodo, iodine

yugular, jugular

Z

zumbido, buzzing

zumbido en los oídos, tinnitus

zurdo, left-handed

ABOUT THE AUTHOR

For more than 25 years, José Luis Leyva has been a translator and interpreter in various technical areas. His vast experience in bilingualism has allowed him to interpret for Presidents, Latin American and US governors, ambassadors, CEO's, judges, prosecutors, forensic experts and healthcare professionals. He is also the author of other books, including technical terminology books of the ***Essential Technical Terminology*** series.

ACERCA DEL AUTOR

Durante más de 25 años, José Luis Leyva se ha desempeñado como intérprete y traductor en diversas áreas técnicas. Su amplia experiencia lingüística lo ha llevado a interpretar para Presidentes de la República, gobernadores latinoamericanos y estadounidenses, embajadores, presidentes de compañías transnacionales, jueces, fiscales, peritos y profesionales del cuidado de la salud. Es también autor de varias obras, entre las que se incluyen los libros de terminología técnica de la serie ***Essential Technical Terminology***.

Made in the USA
Coppell, TX
31 March 2021